CW00960989

STOCK

BB 0316651 1

By the same author

Nice Promises

I Spy in Russia

Tim Sebastian

Chatto & Windus London

For my mother and father

Acknowledgements

My thanks go to BBC Television News for kind permission to publish this book – also to Reg Gallehawk for his patient advice and encouragement with the pictures.

Peter Ruff, Steve Hurst, Ken and Florence Willinger, Robin Gedye, Steve Mallory, Anne McDermid, Jan Dalley, Chip Cheney, Mark Phillips, Joe Ritchey and Greg Amadon deserve special gratitude.

First published in 1986
by Chatto & Windus Ltd
40 William IV Street
London WC2N 4DF

All rights reserved. No part of this publication may be reproduced, stored in a retrieval system or transmitted in any form, or by any means, electronic, mechanical, photocopying, recording or otherwise, without the prior permission of the publisher.

British Library Cataloguing in Publication Data

Sebastian, Tim
   I spy in Russia. *Russia*
1. Soviet Union Social conditions—
   1970–
   I. Title
   947.085'4   HN523.5

   ISBN 0-7011-3158-6

Text and photographs copyright © Tim Sebastian 1986

Printed by
Butler & Tanner Ltd,
Frome, Somerset

ART & DESIGN | 1
CLASS No. 947.088
CAT. 77
DATE 12/9/86
BBC LIBRARY

Contents

Introduction

The journey to Moscow took nearly three years and three and three-quarter hours. The BBC and the Foreign Office helped with the first part and British Airways did the rest.

I had set out in 1981 naïvely expecting that it would be an easier ride, but as the telephone calls multiplied and the letters piled up it was clear that Moscow was more distant than I had imagined. Seasons and birthdays would come and go before the Kremlin was to inch open its door.

Relief came unexpectedly in May 1984, by which time I was barely recognisable from the photo which accompanied the original application. But the Soviet government issued me with the coveted multi-entry visa and the warm glow of welcome seemed to extend outwards from the Kremlin palace itself. It was to last sixteen months.

In September 1985 I was among thirty-one Britons ordered out of Moscow for 'activities incompatible with their status' – a loose diplomatic euphemism for spying. It meant that one sixth of the world's landmass was out of bounds and 280 million of its inhabitants had collectively slammed their door.

It's an anticlimax being thrown out of the USSR. Nobody tears up your visa in front of you, strips you of Soviet possessions or harangues you under a single lightbulb in the basement of the Lubyanka. Instead, a list of the expelled was handed to the British embassy with a comradely three-week stay of execution. Time to pack, to say goodbye and to stare hard into a few faces you won't see again.

For their part Soviet officials received me with politeness, even a sense of humour. 'It's not our fault,' they assured me.

'It's not mine either,' I replied.

The blame for the unpleasant episode was pinned on the

British government, which had seen fit to disrupt the blossoming relationship with Moscow by cheekily expelling some real spies. Moscow was settling the account.

Our Russian acquaintances seemed genuinely sorry, but unsurprised, to see us go. No one, I think, took the accusations seriously. They assumed our expulsion was an act of political reciprocity – which it was.

Regrettably there was little time to collect souvenirs. But I have a signed portrait from Russia's number-one singer Alla Pugachova, the front page of *Pravda* the day Mikhail Gorbachev took power and a crumpled Soviet driving licence, the details handwritten in official black ink, as if a jagged dog's tooth had scratched its way across the page.

Not much to show from a nation of fifteen autonomous republics and six time zones – and yet to have filled my bag with *matryoshka* dolls, deer-skin keyrings, wooden bears and salad spoons would not have constituted a better reflection of Soviet life. For that I have taken away the memory of much hospitality and warmth, all the more welcome for being unexpected. There were sparkling chance encounters and conversations which bridged a human, if not a political, gap. There was also the deadening millstone of petty officialdom. Each contact, each conversation gave a fresh insight. I'd like to have collected more.

It's fashionable to believe that the Russians are a subjugated people, dreaming only of Oxford Street or Fifth Avenue and waiting for Christ to open the borders, but that doesn't hold true. The Soviet government appears to rule with broad public support, not because each citizen had the chance to choose it, but because it accurately reflects their character and aspirations. One of the Russians' striking features remains their desire for conformity: the single concentration on how to cut their cake, and not whether there exists a cake at all.

Soviet power is wielded in a relatively direct fashion compared to that of the West. It's not just in the decrees emanating from the Kremlin, but also in the attitude of the restaurant commissionaire who slams the door in your face because he has the power to do it, or the hotel receptionist who will keep you waiting for half an hour because she doesn't like your face. Those who have power in the Soviet Union use it.

And yet the questioning of that power produces interesting responses. A foreigner quickly learns that, in Russia, the reflex 'no' does not mark the end of a request, it opens the bidding. Russians use the word 'no' to sort the serious from the frivolous.

If you accept it and walk away you aren't really interested. The following conversation took place in a major hotel.

'Do you have any ketchup, please?'

'No, it's finished.'

'Are you telling me that in a big international hotel there isn't one bottle of ketchup?'

'I don't know.'

'But you said there wasn't any.'

This to the woman's disappearing back.

The ketchup arrived five minutes later with no explanation.

A surprising number of things are negotiable in the Soviet Union. The difficulty is recognising those who are authorised to deal. One of the strengths of the Soviet system is that an individual seldom meets the people who make the decisions directly affecting him. The path to power is obscured. It's difficult to argue; you don't know whom to argue with.

One Soviet acquaintance was denied permission to visit the West and told it was not in the best interests of the state. He could never find out who had made that pronouncement, so never knew where to challenge it. The system had covered its tracks.

To be a foreigner in that country is not really to be there at all. You don't live with Russians, shop with Russians or share their hardships. You don't change or affect their lives, colour or influence them in any way at all. Like a birthday, you're a one-off phenomenon with no relation to normal life the rest of the year round. You inhabit a foreigners' compound guarded by the militia, drive a foreign car and frequent a supermarket where American Express does nicely. You are relegated to the sidelines. The one break-out is travel.

I remember arriving at Volgograd airport at 4.30 am for a flight to Moscow. It was still dark. All around were the ghosts of the city's previous incarnation – Stalingrad. We were herded sleepily onto one of the workhorses of the Soviet internal airfleet – a Tupulov 134. There was the inevitable group of schoolchildren and harassed teachers. They lolled half-awake, wishing they were somewhere else, snapping bad-temperedly at each other. I know nothing about flying, but it soon became apparent that this plane wasn't going to do any. The batteries were straining and wheezing but the jets weren't catching. A stewardess admitted defeat.

'You will please disembark and board the neighbouring plane.' A man in his forties, wearing a plastic three-quarter-length coat, leaned across the aisle towards me.

'Good thing this happened down here and not up there.' He grinned a mouthful of gold teeth and pointed upwards.

It was raining on the runway, which did nothing for the passengers' bad temper. Four identical planes were lined up side by side. Perhaps, someone suggested, we would have to try all of them. We clambered aboard a second time, some people praying, others swearing. This plane didn't sound any better. What about a kick start? came a proposal from the back. Everyone laughed. The aircraft seemed to take umbrage.

'We have to refuel,' said the voice on the tannoy.

'What do you mean *refuel*?' everyone asked. 'We haven't gone anywhere.'

It was onto a bus this time. We were cold, tired and rained on. As the sun came up the day appeared lousier by the minute. Half an hour later we were back on board, streaking down the runway, then making a wide arc north into the Moscow flightpath. The man with the gold teeth leaned over again.

'A colleague and I once set out for Moscow from Moldavia. He insisted on flying and I went by train. By the time I arrived he hadn't even left.' He roared with laughter. Part of the joy of Russia.

It was a small piece of the Soviet jigsaw and thankfully

there were many others. Visits to theatres where they subtly mimic former leaders, jazz concerts, private art exhibitions – even joyrides on the Moscow River. The Soviet Union may not encourage a look below the surface, but it rewards the search.

*   *   *

'I suppose you have everything in the West?' It was the hotel floorlady, passing the evening hours behind an enormous desk full of keys and records, her oversize television lecturing the world from a corner.

'If you have money, you can buy most things,' I replied.

She smiled pityingly. 'How boring! No surprises. Every day the same as the one before.'

Russians are told a great deal about the West, and find out quite a bit more. But many of the old, entrenched views prevail. I've met those who believe that Britons need exit visas to leave the country, that the unemployed receive no social benefit, and that the homeless and destitute outnumber the housed and prosperous many times over. In official eyes Western freedom is the freedom to be without a job or a roof, the freedom to sleep on a park bench or to forage in dustbins and to exchange one uncaring society for another if you so desire. None of those freedoms is envied, and many look no further.

But Russians like to be liked and go to enormous trouble to impress foreigners. I remember meeting a family celebrating a wedding anniversary in a Moscow restaurant. Without a second thought they invited me to their flat the next day.

The table was laid, not for tea, but for a banquet. Grandmother and Grandfather were at the door to welcome me – it turned out to be their flat – and the son and daughter-in-law began passing round food and drinks. They were warm and hospitable. We chatted about families, the climate, and peace on earth. Most importantly they were anxious to meet again, they wanted me to like Russia.

'We've never done this sort of thing,' said the daughter-in-law nervously. 'I mean, meeting foreigners. Perhaps you

11

could visit our little country plot outside Moscow.' Perhaps not. It happened to be in a closed area.

The grandmother was a member of the Communist Party, but we avoided speaking of politics. None of us wanted to disagree, to sever the tiny link that held us together. It was a heartening experience but a sad one. Good to meet and talk, but we were aware of how few occasions there are for spontaneous contact. Soviet humour and directness would go down well in the West, if given the chance.

Russians can be bitterly incisive about their own system. They know its faults and weaknesses better than anyone. Perhaps the most revealing catchphrase isn't a joke or an anecdote. It isn't even funny. It's a question, '*Kto kovo*?' which means 'Who does what to whom?' Who's who? Who's on top and who's underneath? These days in Moscow it's hard to tell. Successful Russians are careful Russians.

I recall sitting in my office early one morning and hearing the door open.

'Who's that?' I called out casually. 'Friend or foe?' A Soviet visitor put his face round the door.

'That depends,' he said and then grinned. 'That depends.'

One can only guess at the uncertainties of day-to-day relationships in a relatively closed society. For the animosities and rivalries that lie on the surface in Western countries are obscured in large measure in the Soviet Union. Those who survive and prosper in that political system are likely to be tougher and more astute than many of their Western counterparts.

For the Soviet political school is a hard one. The longer an administration remains in power, the longer the ladder is blocked, the longer the waiting list, the more frustrated the political ambitions.

All the signs were that the accession of Mr Gorbachev in 1985 was accompanied by an easing of the political log jam of a kind not seen for decades. It was the opportunity for a rapid scramble up the stairs and into the Kremlin before the door closed again for another generation.

It was an exciting time to be in Moscow because Russians

began to talk about their new leaders with pride, where before they had avoided mentioning them. These were the early months, when there were new-sounding speeches, walkabouts and foreign appearances in Paris and Geneva, and when the Soviet leader was found to be another Great Communicator, a child of the video age.

The change of style alone was enough to excite many; some felt a change in substance was bound to come later. The final judgement is some way off.

'We've wasted enough time in previous years,' said a commentator at Moscow Television. 'Now perhaps we can get moving. But there is a lot to do.'

It was at the television station that much of our work was conducted. Entrance to the building is heavily restricted by the militia, and foreigners are signed in and out on special passes by members of the International Relations Department.

Fortunately they have a sense of humour. On the wall of their office is the now well-known poster showing Margaret Thatcher in the arms of Ronald Reagan, a nuclear mushroom cloud in the background. The caption reads, 'She promised to follow him to the end of the world. He promised to organise it.' It was a big favourite with the staff.

I think they had a good idea of what our work entailed, and we of theirs. The relationship was very different from the stereotype of Western correspondents hounded by their Soviet minders. They did say no – often forcibly – but they sometimes said yes as well. We even managed to laugh together without political contamination. Perhaps, in a limited way, we surprised each other.

Soviet television is charged with transmitting the most important half-hour of propaganda in the Communist world – the nightly news bulletin *Vremya* (Time). The editor is an amiable, balding man, who was interested enough to ask what I thought of the programme, and to make notes for whatever purpose.

I asked him why they always opened with a home-affairs story.

'It's very simple,' he replied. 'Our position at home dictates our position abroad. If we're strong at home, we're strong on the international scene.'

'You read a lot of very long announcements.'

'I know. We've asked the Central Committee if they couldn't shorten some of them. But you know, we are never going to please everyone. Some people want more of this or that, others want something completely different. You won't find anyone in the Soviet Union who says he likes the news or dislikes it. But they do watch it.'

They certainly do. And you can tell a lot about the Soviet Union by what it does and doesn't say about itself. For example, a prominent member of the Politburo visited a Communist Party congress in Hungary and was accorded less than ten seconds in the film coverage. He was ousted within a year. But the aim of Soviet news is to promote the country in its best or most desirable light, not to show what happened within a given period. Everything has to have a point.

'Aren't you interested in better relations between our two countries?' a Soviet technician asked me one evening.

I explained that that would be a good by-product, but it wasn't my aim to promote or denigrate anything, simply to report.

'So you're aimless,' she replied, 'and you don't care what you do, or say. I don't think that serves the cause of peace.'

There's no room in the Soviet Union for the uncommitted. You're supposed to know where you're going, and if you don't serve the cause it doesn't really count.

However, behind the slogans and the chiselled, angular men and women who stare down from the posters, there's some concern for those who don't measure up. Hiding on the ground floor of a red-brick block of flats in a Moscow suburb, group therapy celebrates its tenth birthday in the Union of Soviet Republics. Even if you know the address it's hard to find the party. The atmosphere is sleepy and clinical, the picture of Lenin on the wall is tiny, and maybe he's closing his ears. For below him a quiet collection of newlyweds is discussing why life is less wonderful than they expected.

A pretty, fast-talking group leader tries to steer them through the emotional minefield. She's in time, for the damage doesn't seem that great – a few couples are even holding hands. And you can't escape the feeling that they've come to try out something new. A shy, thin man in his early thirties comes out of an office in a white coat. Behind him, similarly clad, is a small, plump lady with severe black hair, perhaps ten years older. 'We are the Masters and Johnson of Moscow,' they declare, and start laughing. We listen in on a session. The plump lady tells a beautiful blonde that men sometimes want 'it' more than women. A dark-haired girl wants to know how to come to terms with her parents' divorce. A man doesn't feel his wife is doing enough in the apartment.

Strangely, it all feels fresh and experimental when you hear it in Moscow: the tentative airing of emotional crises, the quiet admission that more help is needed than *Pravda* can offer.

The Soviet Union is not famous for its diversity of thought – rather, the constant emphasis is on a single truth, a theme long evident in Russian culture. There are supporters and opponents, but there are few agnostics. This is a nation of strong opinions.

I was to find that on many occasions. None was more memorable than a visit to a war veteran in the city of Volgograd. He was friendly and hospitable, but his smile turned to an expression of horror when he learned that I represented the British media. 'Why had we poured filth on his country, why did we not tell the truth, why did we continue to desecrate the memories that he and other Russians held dear?'

It's not easy to answer accusations like that over a cup of tea, particularly if the cup belongs to the accuser. You either say 'It's not true' or 'I'm sorry'. But there wasn't much point. The first wouldn't have been believed, and the second was unacceptable to both of us.

It was rare to encounter such open hostility. Russians tend to greet foreigners well, but the foreign media are another matter. It's a useful reminder that only in our own perception are we classified as the Good Boys. To a Russian we are guilty of frequent slander and distortion.

The militiaman charged with keeping us away from a courtroom or demonstration has little or no understanding of why we might be there. To him we are simply troublemakers, upsetting public order and focusing on the criminal and undesirable elements in society – of no possible interest to right-thinking journalists. There is probably equally little reciprocal understanding on our part. Most Russians do not like to see their boat rocked, and an unofficial demonstration is as likely to be broken up by enraged pedestrians as by the police. There is also widespread condemnation for those who want to leave the country and an automatic assumption that they lack patriotism.

'What's wrong with living here?' one woman asked me. 'Why should they want to live somewhere else? We've got mountains, lakes, seas, sun and snow. What else is there?'

*   *   *

There *is* the bath-house – *banya* in Russian – the point where East and West finally divide. It's one of the most traditional forms of masochism on offer to the Soviet public and no self-respecting sadist would be seen in it.

Consider the attractions: multiple, independently-targeted jets of water, a dark-green pool with water apparently un-changed since the Revolution, stone slabs to lie on while your comrade soaps you down from head to foot, and a sauna that cooks your bottom and scrambles your brain in less time than a microwave.

Standing behind every baroque pillar in this unisex col-iseum is a naked figure, wanting nothing more than to beat your back raw with birch twigs, smiling all the time and telling you how clean you've become. If you're tired of your body this is the place to get rid of it.

I only went once and wish I'd had the courage to go again. It's a social occasion as much as a surgical cleaning operation. And you can quite literally go just for the beer. Dressed in a makeshift tent, or nothing at all if you want, your can rent an alcove with a curtain and close yourself off from the communal dressing room. It's a chance to relax with your friends in alcoholic purdah.

Bring a little fish, or look for one in the pool, and you have the makings of a fine indoor picnic. In fact you can take anything you want apart from a person of the opposite sex – bath-houses are segregated – and a camera. And that explains why I have to write about the bath-house instead of showing pictures of it.

Many foreigners get addicted to it; Russians consider it as natural as eating breakfast. To them it's part of a grand communal tradition, togetherness, a collective undertaking in pursuit of a collective goal – the clean human being. It has nothing to do with Communism, for they've been indulging in this pastime longer than anyone can remember, and there's no reason why it should ever stop, even if every Muscovite were to possess his own bathroom. They like doing things together. Provided the water-jets aren't shut down as part of a future arms agreement, they'll continue to do so.

Apart from their baths it's hard to know what matters to Russians. Their traditions, their family, their country – certainly. But what is it that gets them out of bed in the morning and into the factories and schools?

Some of them, it's said, have not been getting out of bed much at all. In recent years the Soviet press has been full of reports of absenteeism and laziness, poor workmanship and parasitism. Strange features in a society with such rigid political guidelines. But the other side of the coin is very different. It pictures a relentless pursuit of excellence, of international recognition and success. Russia in a hurry.

Children who ski down the Lenin Hills on a winter afternoon are doing more than physical jerks. By the age of nine they've been streamed and divided by ability into the 'cans' and 'can'ts' of Soviet society. The 'cans' will be further assessed and promoted. They may go on to specialist schools of sport, where the training and the competition will be intense.

It's similar in the world of ballet. I remember a mother

agonising about whether her daughter should apply to the Bolshoi school. Would she ever see her again? Would there be more than just the occasional weekends together, more than the waving at a performance and the long, long absences? Would this Soviet child become a Soviet success story and a stranger to her parents? Many do.

I've visited special language schools where ten-year-olds speak near-perfect English and chant 'Row, row, row the boat gently down the stream.' They presented an odd sight, sitting in their formal classroom in the middle of Moscow, the walls bedecked with pictures of Big Ben – odder still when they reached the line, 'Life is but a dream.'

I asked one of those privileged, talented children what she wanted most from life. 'Makeup?' I ventured. 'A fur coat, or perhaps a ring or a necklace?'

She paused and looked up at me as if the question had never been put to her before. 'I would like a friend,' she said quietly. 'Just a good friend.'

I barely recognised her outside the school. She had on a woollen cap and a red checked coat. Her shadow was long in the winter evening sunshine as she walked home alone.

*   *   *

To bring out a camera on a Soviet street is to test the limits of society's tolerance. Taking pictures of family and friends is all right, but many Russians consider casual photography an unnatural act – on a par with dropping your trousers in public.

'Where's your permit to film?' is the standard opener from the boys in blue-grey.

'I don't need one. It's a public place with no military installation in sight.'

'You need permission.'

'Then I don't have it.'

You learn early on that the starting point for this discussion is rather different from that in the West. Things in Russia may well be forbidden unless expressly permitted. And while that's a small exaggeration it's a useful guide to anyone wielding a camera. If the militia don't get you, the old *babush-ki*, the grandmothers, will.

'Why are you taking pictures?' one of them asked me on Gorky Street.

'Why not?'

'But why? There has to be a reason. You have no right to take pictures without a reason.'

Ah, the subject of rights! They are never far below the surface, especially where photographs are concerned. You cannot photograph bridges, stations, airports, phone boxes or wires of any description. Difficult in a city which still runs trams.

You don't miss much by keeping away from bridges and airports, but the stations would make wonderful pictures. They offer biblical scenes of colour, each journey an exodus, each station a bazaar. At night people sit sleeping in the vast stone halls. Some mill around eating slabs of sweating cheese or salami made from spiced fat. I've seen men and women lie on the floor, their children on top of them, their boxes and baskets alongside. Army recruits wander about in small groups. Some queue for tickets, others for medicine or sandwiches. They leave when they can.

You can't photograph them because stations are strategic objects.

So in no sense is this a complete book, rather a collection of photographic impressions, a reflection of the small part of the Soviet Union I was able to see. I have tried to omit the familiar and include the unusual: there are no Olympic medallists or ballet dancers, no smiling, committed factory workers, and only one famous achiever.

The people differ from Westerners in almost every way. Their aims and ideals are radically different, as are their knowledge, their outlook on the world and their perception of their own identity. Not much of that may be visible from these pictures, but I hope some of it is.

It's impossible to remain indifferent to the Soviet Union, to its size, its power or its people. 'We're like the climate,' they tell you. 'Very hot or very cold. You notice us.'

Thinking back it's the little memories that stick: like the official in the Arctic city of Murmansk who gave up his evening to drive through the snowscape to the airport to bring us champagne and bars of chocolate. He didn't say much, just smiled and waved and waved. It was May, fifteen degrees below, and he wore a thick coat and fur hat. To him summer was a word in a dictionary.

In fact most of those memories have snow in them. Frozen rivers, trees weighed down with ice, traffic police in thick black sheepskins, their faces raw from the wind, snowdrifts that come up to the thigh, the morning miracle of starting the car, technology against climate, boots in the hall.

Six months have passed since I left Moscow, and the Kremlin goes about its business visibly unhindered by the loss of six British correspondents. I'd like to go back, but that's improbable. The Russians withdrew their invitation and may not renew it. All the same it seems appropriate to send my regrets.

Tim Sebastian
Washington D.C.
April 1986

1

Dog Day

If a Soviet dog is Soviet man's best
friend, then these two are
stretching the friendship. Imagine
living in a communal flat with
them. They were the heroes at
Moscow's bi-annual dog show, as
viciously contested as any human
competition. The dark, unfriendly
stares aren't just for the camera:
they're the real thing. If you can't
win with your looks, you have a go
with your teeth.

The Russians don't just go silly
about their dogs, they go
downright mad, weighing them
down with medals and carting
them off to distant dog shows in
one-horse towns.

Unlike the human gatherings, there were no political speeches and no slogans about peace. This was a day for naked ambition, showing what you have and flaunting it. Just a few of the four-legged prestige symbols of Soviet society.

Between events they sold gut-crushing hunks of *shaslik* – widely believed to originate from last year's losers. But there wasn't even vodka to calm the contestants' nerves.

The Russians wanted to know what dog shows in Britain are like. But how do you explain about tea and sandwiches at Crufts, and the pampered canine class in the West? This crowd – Nogush, Lavrik, Lorinat and many others – would eat them alive.

2

Winter and the Rest

Even Moscow has its share of chocolate-box pictures. This is the children's treat at the capital's zoo. In winter it's a refined sort of treat – more like an Outward Bound exercise. The children don three layers of clothing. The animals get half a layer. Most of them can't be cajoled out of their cages at any price. I couldn't escape the feeling that we were mentally deranged being there at all. Only the horse seemed unconcerned.

Let me introduce spring inside the Arctic Circle – a region that the Czars declared too hostile for even the birds to settle.

Murmansk is now a special city, with some of the best-paid, best-housed people in the Soviet Union. Salaries are at least double the national average, there's extra holiday, and a greater variety of food than in many other areas. But it's still a hard climb from the centre to the flats above the town. The people of Murmansk deserve their privileges. They live through months of Arctic night, and there is little choice of work – the majority of the town is involved with the Soviet Navy or the fishing industry.

In summer they call it the 'Town without Children' as the young are transported en masse to the Black Sea resorts to remind them what the sun looks and feels like. It's easy to forget.

While the West blames the East for its cold weather, the Russians can only blame themselves. Winter is the real season, the rest is just time in between. In Russia preparations for winter occupy much of the people's time, and much of the State's money. It's known as the Arctic tax. Every summer Muscovites lose their hot water for about six weeks, while the city's centralised heating system is serviced.

At three pm on a winter's day in Moscow, the temperature is minus twenty, and someone has gone fishing. Not that the river has much else to offer. In the background stands the Ukraine hotel, which looks only a few degrees more welcoming than the weather.

It looked a bit like 'The Day of the Triffids', but it was just a normal winter day on the Lenin Hills. The Russians place sacks over the bushes to protect them from the cold, part of a growing environmental protection movement.

I'm not sure if it's the same movement that has placed imitation plastic deer and bears along some of the country roads outside the city. Perhaps they hope Russians will leave the 'real thing' alone. It may be too late. This luckless bear ended up stuffed in the window of a hunting shop, just four blocks from the Lubyanka. He seemed to draw plenty of customers, for hunting has no shortage of enthusiasts in the Soviet Union. I knew one hunter who used to take to the woods at the weekend and return full of raucous stories about the bears tiptoeing up behind him and tapping him on the shoulder. It was his explanation of why he never hit one.

In Moscow the winters are so long that there isn't any time to lose. It takes only a weak ray of sunshine to get the Russians out of their clothes and offering their bodies to the fully suspecting world. At lunch-time along the Moscow River you bring your food with you. They may have many burdens in life – but inhibitions are not among them. The Western obsession with dieting has yet to take hold in Russia. In fact a diet is widely considered a licence to eat!

It's a holiday camp without the beds. Plenty of slick comic entertainment, with a fast-talking compère and a group of willing victims. His job is to make a fool of them in public, and their job is to enjoy it. They all do what's expected of them. The Russians have made a culture of jokes – *anekdoty* – and the laughter is given freely.

I was singled out to be one of the judges for a singing competition. I'm ashamed to say I sloped off back to the beach before the competition finished. I fancied I knew who the next victim was going to be!

Moments of togetherness, Soviet-style, along the inland waterways outside the capital. The lakeside resort, named the Bay of Joy, is a favourite with Muscovites and foreigners. This was keep-fit in a clearing, dancing to the jaunty thump of Moscow Radio on a loudspeaker.

Summer died that afternoon. It was wet, windy and the wrong end of September. A chill wind seemed to have dropped in from Siberia for a month or six, but some people never give up.

The woman in the picture had paid for her deck chair and was damned if she wasn't going to use it. Her bottom was probably the last in Moscow to see ultraviolet light for a whole season.

The notice beside her carried a salutary warning: 'Swimming in an unsober state is dangerous.'

You have to tell some people everything.

3

Streets Ahead

A placard, a symbol and a slogan for every occasion. And politics everywhere you turn.

Poster art has been popular and sophisticated for many years, but size is everything. Man dwarfed by the message. The individual placed in his collective context.

Lenin, never knowingly speechless, quoted here on the wall of a theatre: 'Of all the arts, the cinema is the most important.' A woman pastes up posters for the 1985 exhibition of scientific and technological progress. And, a full five years after the Olympic games, Misha, the ubiquitous Russian symbol for the competition, obstinately refuses to leave public life.

Kalinin Prospekt is the pride of
Moscow, built as a showpiece with
high-rise office blocks and shops
that stay open late.

The Kremlin leadership gets
this view every day as they streak
down the centre lane on their way
home from the office.

In Moscow I used to miss the bright lights of the West: now I miss the dim lights and the feeling of power and intrigue I could sense at night in Moscow.

This is the top end of Gorky Street, the main thoroughfare which takes you from the city centre straight out to the international airport.

It's midnight and the traffic jams are long over, but the empty streets are deceptive. Traffic police are stationed at regular intervals along all major roads, day and night. They are polite and insistent, and the breathalyser equipment is well up to date.

The slightest sign of alcohol and you can lose your licence. That, at least, is the theory. A Ukrainian newspaper reported that if police took all the drunk drivers off the road, industry would be at a standstill within days. Clearly the authorities exercise their discretion.

One curious rule for driving at night: no headlights can be used except in emergency. Sidelights only. Headlights are for important people.

Another typical Moscow
silhouette – the Stalinist wedding
cake. A handful of them were
dotted with brutal generosity
around Moscow. They
represented the fashion of the

Fifties, designed to impress and overawe. Stalin tried giving one or two to the other East European states, but the gesture wasn't appreciated.

They serve as useful landmarks in a city where so many roads look the same.

This one was thought to serve other purposes as well. Situated just a few hundred yards from the US embassy, it's believed to be discreetly adorned with listening devices to keep one superpower in tune with the other.

The reason for the picture – nothing sinister. I was stuck in a traffic jam and couldn't miss it.

Just one of the dozens of 'micro-regions' in Moscow – the dormitory suburbs that house the capital's workforce.

Life out there is not always fun – and that is official. City authorities have complained about inadequate transport and long delays in the housing programme.

A number of officials have been sacked recently for incompetence.

Normally each housing estate is served by a supermarket, but the supplies can be erratic. Nevertheless the suburbs are deceptive. This housing estate supports a semi-official theatre,

one or two makeshift art galleries and a number of unofficial music groups. There are no advertisements or brightly coloured signs. Soviet pleasures take some finding. No signposts to the fun. Like so much that goes on in Moscow, you just have to know.

The view from our apartment.

In Moscow we were citizens of the Timiryazevski Region, one of the northern suburbs near the Television Tower. And enjoyed it. It conferred on us a view of a building site, the best dairy shops in the capital, and a small mental institution just around the corner, which might one day have come in handy. There were also some of the best parks and sunsets in Eastern Europe. It was a friendly, bustling area, and the foreigners' compound sat strangely in the middle of it.

Perhaps the best aspect of our living conditions was the caretaker, a lady in her late sixties, whose humour and kindness had survived intact. She treated us a little like marooned Martians – to be looked at with curiosity and fussed over. But carrying, perhaps, some contagious interplanetary disease.

'We want you to be happy,' she would say continually. 'Anything you want and we shall do it for you.' Then she would laugh and wander off shaking her head.

She didn't want her picture taken, so I settled for the view from her building instead.

I had just started to believe I spoke Russian when I travelled in this man's taxi. Every fifth word was unintelligible and I could just make out where one slang expression ended and the other began. In the end I said to him, 'Do you mind if I take your picture as a souvenir?'

'Yes, I do,' he replied.

But by then I had taken it. I got out of the taxi with him wishing me what I took to be much bad luck in the future.

Like New York, Moscow has yellow taxis, but Moscow's are cheaper.

This one was heading north to the Television Tower – but the child in the back looked as if she had her mind on other things.

Most Moscow taxi journeys take place in silence – drivers rarely exchange pleasantries or even say goodbye. Sometimes it's difficult to know whether or not they have heard your destination.

'How much longer?' I asked one of them.

'We'll arrive later today,' came the reply.

The head didn't move, but I could swear the lips parted.

The design is from the Fifties, the engineering pre-war, the owner delighted. For Soviet cars were built to last. Like dinosaurs, the older models should have become extinct, but the Russians lavish on them so much care and attention, so much ingenuity, that they survive the winters other cars can't.

Many of them hibernate for the winter. They're locked up in the dozens of car compounds scattered throughout the major cities. They're dressed in tarpaulins, their tyres go flat, and the whole package is left rotting till the spring, when the owner returns, desire and energy refreshed.

Buying a new car is quite an experience in the Soviet Union. Forget the bright showrooms, the silver-tongued salesmen and the promise of discounts and dependability – imagine instead a fenced-off compound with a pensioner guarding the gate. A friend took up the story.

'I've come to collect my new car.'

'Uh?'

'My new car!'

'Papers.'

'Here they are.'

'Go and choose the colour you want. They're over there.'

At the moment only one in twenty-eight Soviet people owns a car, compared to an average of one in three in Western Europe. But there is pressure to increase domestic production. A car, said one Soviet magazine, improves the quality of life, and should be regarded as beneficial. Times, it seems, are changing.

Make someone happy . . . don't phone. It looks easy enough. The calls are cheap and the boxes aren't vandalized. But the problems begin later. There aren't any phone books!

In general the only directories are for official organisations and severely restricted.

The major problem in telephoning any organisation is the absence of a central switchboard. Each department, and sometimes each employee has a different external number. If the person you want is out, there's a good chance no one else will pick up the receiver. Frustrating? Unbelievably. The usual scenario is that a phone rings unanswered for half the day, and then remains engaged for the rest.

Small wonder that Soviet businessmen take trips where their Western counterparts make phone calls. It isn't good enough just to ring up, you have to turn up and solve the problem in person.

Among the worst places to call are the major hotels. If you're trying to telephone a friend or visitor for a quick meal . . . forget it. By the time you locate them it's probably the next day.

The contrast is the international operators, slick, polite and highly expensive.

This statue in Tallinn, Soviet Estonia, seems to be the kind of humour Russians enjoy. A boy and girl shelter with an umbrella, but the water comes up from below and the umbrella is useless. I was sure there was a message in that, but I'm probably mistaken.

One of my abiding memories of Russia.

Some of the older trucks were notoriously unreliable. I remember seeing statistics showing that they cost almost as much to repair during their working life as they do to manufacture in the first place. This is hardly surprising, since they have to perform in an extreme climate, and frequently on poor roads.

The older models have no heater in the cab so the drivers swig vodka to keep warm in winter. Muscovites are always wary of them: you never know on which side of the road they'll be driving – until they hit you.

The more dignified Leningrad
sphinx is from another era.

It's just any old queue, and there were plenty to choose from. It was difficult to get permission to film inside a shop.

On arrival in Moscow an official asked me, 'Why should we let you take pictures in our stores? You would only say that there's no food in them.'

I think we both changed our attitudes. The authorities became less sensitive about queues, and we less preoccupied with them.

I don't know if anyone ever let this lady in. She was waiting outside a 'Voters' Club', just off Gorky Street, a few weeks before elections to the Supreme Soviet, the country's national assembly.

Once inside she would have heard speeches about the duty of voting and policy submissions from the different candidates, in essence read-outs from *Pravda*. She could have put down her bags and rested her feet and taken part in the only grass-roots political movement, offered by the Communist Party.

Not all candidates are elected. The principal struggle is to get *selected*. For that you require backing from a factory or trade union. Individuals cannot make it on their own – anywhere.

'It may not be the sort of democracy you are used to,' one Soviet journalist told me, 'but it works here. We believe that the goal of society is unity, instead of wasting time and energy while a lot of different parties haggle amongst each other. We went through all that.'

'Everyone to the polling station,' says the sign by the door. And they do mean everyone.

4

Face Up

Mid-morning in a courtyard in central Moscow. The grandmothers – the *babushki* – rule Russia from courtyards like this, sheltering in winter, sitting out gossiping in the summer. Each year they spend many months arguing about the severity of the winter. They claim to feel it in their bones, and most of them do. How do they cope with winter?

'Shake and move a lot,' said one old lady.

'Bathe every morning in cold water from top to bottom,' came another reply.

It's worth listening to them, for the women of the Soviet Union have a reputation for surviving.

A million people died in the siege of Leningrad during the Second World War – and most of them were men. The women could always carry on longer.

And nowadays they salute old age, particularly in women. As the saying goes, '*Vsorok pyat, baba yagodka opyat*': 'at forty-five a woman becomes a berry again.' Just a coincidence, I suppose, that berries tend to be red.

Two faces from the gambling
Mafia at the Moscow race track –
the Hippodrome: the only place in
the Soviet Union where Lenin
looks away and allows legal
betting.

Very few people wanted their
picture taken, because they had
told their wives they were
somewhere else.

Here, though, the class system
makes an unexpected
appearance: 30 kopeks for the
stands, 80 for the enclosure.

From Russia with . . . Love in Red
Square

Viveka, who lived in Tallinn,
coped with us for three days and
survived with her humour intact.
She epitomised the relaxed new
breed in the Baltic republics. First
language: Estonian; second
language: accented Russian. It's a
region of conflicting signals, at
least from the television, for
Western television adverts beam
in strongly across the gulf of
Finland, and Finnish is widely
understood. There's a strange
irony, watching Capitalist
television in Communist Russia. No
cut price chickens or washing
machines here.

Eating out in Russia *is* an experience. This is the Berlin, one of the finest restaurants in the capital, complete with pre-Revolutionary decor and post-Revolutionary vodka.

There's no ready welcome at a Soviet restaurant. Almost every establishment carries a sign in the window: *Full Up*. To surmount it there are three choices: use money or influence, pay in hard currency, or decide on a long wait.

Fast food in Russia is what happens to it when it appears. It's not the process beforehand.

The food is often exotic – chicken crushed between bricks is an interesting starting point – but you go more in the expectation of Soviet company than gastronomic delights. A restaurant is a good place to destroy barriers. I have begun several meals in Moscow hostelries which were completed some hours, or days, later in a Russian flat.

Sunday afternoon in the Moscow inner city. The capital's trend-setters have almost finished with skate-boarding: break-dancing is the new craze.

Moscow rewards a stroll in the back streets. Sadly, for every half-decent picture taken, a thousand better images flash past unnoticed. There's a lazy stillness about Moscow at the weekend. The people stand around in courtyards, idle on the streets, air their winter coats on sunny balconies, sing songs and play their accordians. Time off from the Revolution.

It was Saturday afternoon on the happiest day of their lives. Bride, bridegroom and friends had come straight from the Palace of Weddings to the Lenin Hills – a traditional pilgrimage for newlyweds. They had just promised to respect the important and socially useful institution of marriage, and were ushered out to do their duty. Normally they crack open champagne, but I seem to have photographed the one group that didn't have any.

While the sun may have shone for them, the statistical chances of their happiness were rather less auspicious. Soviet marriages are breaking up, I was told, not because of hardship, but because the hardship is coming to an end.

'When couples have to struggle,' said one sociologist in Moscow, 'they stay together. When they get a bit richer, get a car and a flat and things are going well, that's the time when the marriage falls apart.'

Most of those in the picture thought I was going to sell it to them. Only the young lady on the left seems to have seen through me.

At the Easter market at Cheryomushkinskoye in Moscow, you can find private merchants from all over the Soviet Union, anxious to talk and to ask questions. Some travel hundreds of miles to market, staying with friends or families, selling for a few days or weeks and returning home across Russia. The modern nomads. They charge whatever they think they can get. It's said that the poorer their clothes, the richer they are.

So much of the Soviet Union carries the image of a grey people enmeshed in a grey bureaucracy. So much of the country is different. Why should the state tolerate Easter markets, how is it there are gypsies, how do they keep their riches, why is private enterprise alive and well on the streets? Just a few Russian surprises.

They're not talking about love, music, clothes or even politics. The two young women are telling each other's fortune from the coffee grains poured into a saucer. Their prospects looked bright for they spent most of the afternoon giggling.

It was a small café on Dmitrovskoye Chaussée, one of the main arterial roads leading into the centre of the capital. As at many other places, the queue outside was the only visible sign of life inside. A Russian friend pushed his way to the front of the queue with two rouble notes in his hand. A hurried, whispered exchange took place with the doorman. We were told to go to the courtyard at the back of the building. There we climbed through a downstairs window, the bribe changed hands and we found ourselves in the café, the only one in the area. Like the other patrons, we counted ourselves lucky to be there.

The clientèle in the cafés is mostly female. Women heavily outnumber men in the Soviet Union and most people frequent the cafes for a purpose. It didn't look like romance at every table, but maybe the coffee grains gave reason to hope.

It's remarkable how much peace can be found along the banks of the Moscow River, well inside the city boundaries. In a society which sets out to organise its people from morning till night and cradle to grave, there seems to be a strong desire for solitude.

Sometimes the 'rest zones' are fenced off, guarded by an old woman in a white coat, whose function is to rent out the weighing machine and charge you the token two-kopek entrance fee. More often than not the woman deserts her post and the peace of Russia is given away for nothing.
I counted these areas among the great 'finds' of Moscow.

Does she have special powers? Is she a witch or a scientist? Did she treat Leonid Brezhnev (unsuccessfully)?

Djuna sidesteps questions like that. She says she just wants to help people. And on Saturday afternoons at her flat in the old Arbat district of Moscow, they queue for the privilege.

What is certain is that she is a faith healer with a remarkable following. She has both credentials and contacts. She assists research into paranormal phenomena at the Academy of Sciences, writes poetry, collects icons and lays her hands on the mighty and powerful of the Soviet Union.

Djuna Davitashvili, to give her full name, is an Assyrian who came to Moscow some seven years ago. She likes media attention and her main consulting room is fitted with television lights to help the foreign networks who tramp through the flat in search of Alternative Moscow. She is that.

'Sit down.'

I did.

'You have recently had an operation,' she informed me. 'I felt the energy move across my face. Am I right?'

She was. Djuna smiled comfortingly. The words 'of course' hung in the air.

'You should be able to feel some warmth.' She had her hand over mine, not touching, but attempting to pass me some energy – a difficult task at the best of times. I thought I felt something, but now I'm not so sure.

'I'm having problems finding a flat in Moscow,' I told her.

'It will be all right,' she replied. 'You will come and live with us.' She was right for a while.

How about global predictions? 'I have looked into the future,' she said, 'and I see good things. There will be peace, not war.'

In the winter of 1984 that was the most upbeat voice I heard in the Soviet capital.

Vladimir Lomeiko is charged with the role of 'front man' for the Soviet foreign ministry, facing Western journalists at the now frequent press briefings. His role consists of reacting to world events (something Moscow used not to bother to do), delivering statements on foreign policy and disguising his exasperation with the questions. Mostly he performs skilfully, knowing exactly when to wrap up a meeting. 'Gentlemen, I would not wish to keep you any longer from your weekend,' was a favourite exit line for a Friday afternoon.

Everything under control. We
didn't know it then, but Mikhail
Gorbachev was already running
the country, standing in for
Konstantin Chernenko who spent
most of his leadership tenure time
lying down sick. I don't know if this
was a farewell kiss or a last-minute
exchange of secrets. Perhaps it
was both. Very Russian.

There are no simple goodbyes in the Soviet Union. Certainly not to a member of the Politburo – and least of all to this member. This little turnout was arranged for Mikhail Gorbachev, on his departure to London in 1984. As dictated by protocol the line-up includes a member of the British embassy staff.

The Russians are masters of the formal occasion. I remember a Polish official complaining bitterly that Communists spent all their time at airports, waving – but it never bothered anyone in Moscow. The better the send-off, the more important the person. It's not entirely unknown for a Soviet politician to leave his post for a visit abroad and to find it occupied when he returns.

No worries here; Mr Gorbachev is firmly in charge.

5

The Entertainers

These two have made it.

Singer Alla Pugachova is talking from her heart in her Moscow flat while her composer Ilya Reznik makes the *pelmyeni* (ravioli) for lunch.

They had got up late after an all-night party. 'You should have seen the number of champagne bottles,' she told me.

It's a pleasant flat in a modern block, with a wary caretaker on the door and a handful of fans that wait outside in all weathers.

'Fans are OK,' says Alla. 'You get tired of seeing their faces, but it would be worse if they weren't there.'

That from the Soviet Union's No 1 star, now cutting her 150 millionth disc after nearly 20 years at the top.

'I'm a purely Russian phenomenon. That's why I'm popular. Other singers are Ukrainian, Estonian, from Central Asia, Jews or whatever . . . but I'm Russian.'

She is direct, confident and assertive. She can afford to be. She used to take tea with the Brezhnev family in their exclusive Kutuzovsky apartment, but she says she knows nothing about politics and isn't interested.

'We don't have time for that sort of thing,' she says.

'Are you rich?'

'I'm not poor.' She shrugs. 'We measure things in a different way here. I get 44 roubles a concert – that's enough to make anyone laugh . . . 44 roubles!' (One rouble to £1 is the official exchange rate; unofficially, it's three to one.) There's a little snort, as only a star can do it.

'But the flat costs pennies, I don't have to provide instruments for the group, and I have a black Mercedes. So there you are.'

Alla Pugachova didn't seem to like us when we arrived, but by the time we left, there were souvenirs in our hands and an invitation to come back for lunch the next day.

She meant it, and I did.

She delighted the crowds at the
Uzbekistan restaurant in Moscow,
and seemed surprised that anyone
should want to take her picture.

It was a good repertoire, half-
English, half-Russian and
delivered with great enthusiasm.
Moscow has a band of restaurant
singers who are relatively free to
choose what they perform – this
singer seemed especially to like
the Beatles' 'Yesterday'.

'I'm ashamed of my English,' she
said when I requested a song. 'But
I listen to Tina Turner and I like
her.'

'You seem very popular here.'

'I don't think so, but I hope they
enjoy themselves.' She really
cared. It certainly wasn't the
money. In the Soviet Union it
rarely is.

It didn't look much, but it sounded wonderful. It was a private jazz concert for a students' union, unadvertised and severely restricted to members.

Had they known about it, hundreds of people might have queued half the day to get in, but a few feet away on the street they walked past unaware that anything was happening. It's typical of many performances in the Soviet Union. Sometimes a concert will be held in virtual secrecy because no one can be found to authorise the publicity leaflets.

These artistes had written their own rock opera, which they performed free and for the pleasure of the few. They are part of the artistic demi-monde, half-sanctioned, half-known, half-fulfilled. Lively, active, but reaching just a small proportion of their potential audience.

I remember being struck by one concert in the suburbs. When it was over the audience sent a delegation onto the stage to offer their most prized token of appreciation. It was mid-winter and it turned out to be an object of some rarity in Moscow – a bunch of bananas.

6

Life with Art

It's not what you expect to find in a communal Moscow flat, but Tanya and her daughter Natasha live with one of the more interesting private picture collections dotted around the city.

Tanya is an art critic, well known among Moscow's intelligentsia. Her two-room flat is a sorting house for modern art, a semi-permanent exhibition.

I remember her with much warmth for her hospitality and her direct, very Soviet humour.

'I'm not sensitive about my pictures. If you don't like them, say so.'

Gennady was showing me his makeshift exhibition of some two hundred drawings that he'd brought with him from Leningrad. He was displaying them in his aunt's flat on the outskirts of Moscow, and he would invite guests to private viewings.

Quiet-spoken and self-effacing, Gennady offered tea and biscuits.

'Could you please be quick? I don't really like having my picture taken.'

I never bought a picture from him but he did give me one – as a 'sign of friendship'. He called it 'City Landscape'. It was very different from the view looking out of that Moscow flat. All around were uniform blocks, stretching out beyond the southern suburbs. The picture is a series of geometric shapes suggesting a church and trees, in soft colours and easy to live with.

7

After a Fashion

Gifted designer, entertainer, comedian and Moscow socialite, Slava Zaitsev is one of the more colourful figures to decorate Moscow society. Foreign embassies court him, politicians' wives are said to fawn on him, and the Moscow public falls in love with him three times a week. That's the frequency of his fashion shows at the House of Fashion on Moscow's Avenue of Peace. Ninety minutes of unique escapism, the sporting of clothes that no respectable Party man would dare to be seen dead in.

Zaitsev knows that, and so do his audiences, and that's where the humour lies. He tells them that the three men wearing a cross between a Robin Hood tunic and a maternity outfit are just meeting for a normal Sunday morning chat on Gogol Boulevard, and they all howl with laughter.

He advises the women on their makeup and the models on their diet.

'My models,' he declares, 'are always hungry and they eat an enormous amount.'

'Why are they so thin?'

'They worry. All models worry. It goes with the job.'

Zaitsev puts a little fun into a lot of lives. But there's a serious side as well. He represents the Soviet version of the American dream.

As the public shuffle out onto the streets after the shows, maybe some of them are dreaming that it might all come true.

It's not quite the everyday look in downtown Leningrad. In fact the only thing that was Soviet was the fur. The models were from Scandinavia, the architecture belonged to the Czars and the scene was arranged by the largest of the American fur retailers.

The company's publicity team took over parts of the city to shoot their promotion pictures for 1986. Leningrad stopped and stared.

It was late summer and the city's hundredth fur auction was gathering speed. Some of the most affluent capitalists in the world were buying fur to drape around Capitalist women, and the Soviets wanted nothing more than to send them home happy.

The merchants knew each other and the auctioneers knew them. Some of the buyers had been coming to Leningrad for forty years. They threw parties and fashion shows for each other, shook hands, got drunk and wished each other peace. Peace, they said, meant good business. 'And let us not forget why we are here.'

None of them did. The Russians trawled in several hundred million more dollars, and the buyers collected the only raw sable the world has to offer.

There wasn't an animal rights campaigner in sight.

8

More about War and Peace

'Peace and security to all nations.' It's hard to walk a hundred yards in Moscow, listen to the radio for five minutes or skim through a newspaper without encountering the word 'peace'. We want peace, we demand peace, don't take away our peace. They chant it like a prayer. Moscow is gripped by the peace fever.

This was an open meeting, organised by the local branch of the Soviet Peace Committee, in a hall near the Lenin Stadium, filled, like most Soviet events, to capacity. The people might have turned up spontaneously but it seems likely that their trade unions recommended attendance.

It was different from a Western meeting. There was no debate and no audience participation, although some gatherings allow it. Instead, a series of speeches proclaiming the peaceful character of Soviet policies, and denouncing Western aggression. What some people call the 'unity ritual'. You lend your body and your applause to the state, thereby strengthening its power and legitimacy. *You* form the majority, to which the will of the minority is subordinated.

In general the meetings impart little new information. They repeat known positions. The key words are attendance, acceptance and obedience.

I arrived late and was told by a woman at the gate that I had no right to enter. 'If you can't come on time,' she said, 'you shouldn't be here. We don't want disturbances.' It took time to find a gate with no female guard, but it was worth the effort.

The Soviet Army is constantly on the move. Day and night the lorries rumble through Moscow into the suburbs. The military form the largest workforce in the country, doing everything from road-building and cutting hedgerows to bringing in the harvest.

Only once was I invited to talk to Soviet soldiers. It was in East Germany, and the Russians were pulling out a tank division in a much publicised display of goodwill to the West.

'Did you like it here?' I began.
'Yes.'
'How long were you here?'
'For the period of our mission.'
I tried again.
'Where are you going now?'
'We will go where our country commands.'
Very well trained!

They call them *nashy rebyata* – 'our boys' – and each Soviet family has at least one. More than the Communist Party the Soviet Army – the former Red Army – unifies Soviet youth and commands wide respect.

This was Sunday morning in Leningrad shortly before the major celebrations marking the fortieth anniversary of the end of the Second World War, and the commanding officer couldn't resist a drill with an audience. He was less keen about cameras, and asked us to expose our film. Our guide reminded him that all events on the open streets in non-military areas can be photographed. The officer argued but gave in.

One of the advantages of Soviet regulations is that there are so many of them, no one can know them all. Even an army officer will hesitate when quoted a rule that he doesn't know.

Our guides were frequently unwilling to be ordered around by men in uniform. I remember one heated conversation in Moscow when a militiaman approached with something unpleasant on his mind.

'Follow me. You have no right to be here.'

'I'm not in the army,' said the guide. 'You can't tell me what to do. And anyway, why are you so rude?'

It stopped the official in his tracks. He seemed as surprised as we were. Perhaps a few small battles are being won out on the streets.

A small corner and a very foreign field. These are British graves, just a handful in a tiny cemetery on a hillside overlooking the Arctic city of Murmansk. They are a reminder of a few of the thousands of British seamen who died in the Arctic convoys taking supplies to the Russians at the height of the Second World War.

The graves are well tended and the city authorities still pay tribute to British assistance. The chairman of the town council produced a book to show that the Soviet Union had awarded Clementine Churchill a special Order of the Red Banner for her fund-raising on behalf of the Soviet war effort.

'We remember the brave British fighters and the help they gave us,' he said formally. And he meant it.

9

In State

There's a saying in the Soviet Union: 'The hardest thing to predict is the past.' And that explains why the people are as secretive about the dead as about the living. History has shown them that you don't have to be alive to fall in or out of favour.

This grave belongs to the disgraced leader Nikita Khrushchev, considered by the West to be exceptionally outgoing, and disdained by those of his countrymen who didn't like anyone to be different.

His remains lie in a part of Moscow's Novodevichy cemetery normally closed to the public. Once a year, on 8 May, this section is opened to select members of the public and relatives in honour of the anniversary of the end of the Second World War.

In February 1985 I applied to the Moscow city authorities to film there on that date. They turned me down. The day before the anniversary they changed their mind. And so, our documents carefully checked by uniformed militia on the gate, we were able to pass through.

Russians seem fascinated by death and the visitors that day were wide-eyed, for the gravestones carried names rarely heard or mentioned in Soviet life: Stalin's widow is buried there, as are poets, authors and politicians going back generations. One stone carried the name 'Robinson Crusoe', but without explanation.

105

They may not hope for the life everlasting, but a grateful state will at least provide a slot in a wall. For special service in the military there is even a missile or model tank to adorn the grave.

That may seem strange in the West, but in a country with 5 million men permanently under arms, the Soviet preoccupation with the military is more understandable. No family is without ties to the armed forces, and to serve as an officer is regarded as a prestige profession.

The Soviet army is widely respected in the West. It is known to employ highly sophisticated tacticians and commanders. Confidence is impressive, and Soviet soldiers are taught to believe they are capable of anything.

But more than one veteran complained to me about the lack of commitment and discipline among the young. Sometimes, he said, he took a stick to his grandson, because the boy's parents were too soft.

'It's not like that in England,' he added. 'There you still have proper discipline. Children are strictly brought up, just as they should be.'

Many Soviet women are more than happy to see their husbands or sons begin their military service. For the Soviet male has taken a bashing in recent years. 'I don't know any real men,' one Soviet woman was heard to say in a queue. 'They get drunk, they don't want to work or take any responsibility.'

In fact even Soviet sociologists say they're trying to give men back the ability to take decisions. One told me, 'For years they expected the state to do everything for them, and it did. Now things are changing. They have to help themselves.'

In Russia the mechanics and ritual of death owe much to the Orthodox church.

People come to the cemeteries to recite eulogies much as they intone prayers in the West. Perhaps some of them do that as well, as they wander among the graves.

The Soviet drive for equality has produced its own potted philosophy. *My vsye budyem tam* – 'We all get there in the end.' 'There' means the wall or the grave, although many Russians jerk a finger towards the sky as they say it.

Only one man is said to have survived death in the Soviet Union. And he's inside his own mausoleum beside the Kremlin wall, embalmed, and decidedly photo-shy.

The slogan – Lenin lived, Lenin lives, Lenin will live – is taught in schools throughout the fifteen republics, part of the elaborate Communist catechism that has replaced religious doctrine.

The memory of Lenin is maintained with the utmost formality in Red Square, where the elite Kremlin guard goose-steps to and from the Lenin Mausoleum on every hour of every day.

The Soviet people may not have ready access to their government, but they can feel the trappings of power. As elsewhere, a simple guard change stands for unwavering continuity and political stability. It matters not that behind the great Kremlin wall the leadership may be struggling to elect (or dismiss) a leader, change a policy (or find one), lend (fraternal) assistance or remove it: none of this should be visible to the outside. And little of it is.

In May 1985 the war veterans came in their thousands to the tomb of the Unknown Soldier in Red Square.

No one remained indifferent to the anniversary. Each veteran, it seemed, had kept his uniform, his photographs and mementos, passing the legends from generation to generation.

Young children can recite the official history of battles and campaigns. And their tears are free and genuine as they do it. I remember talking to a group of students throwing stones in the Volga. What did they think of America?

'America is bad and aggressive,' they replied.

'And England?'

'England is our friend and our wartime ally.'

We met many veterans and no one refused us hospitality and in many cases it was lavish. Whatever their personal attitude to the West, they all asked us to convey one message.

'Tell the world that the Soviet soldier wants peace.'

I pass it on word for word, as requested.

They looked at Nikita
Khrushchev's grave for just a
moment and then turned their
back on it. They had other
memories to discuss. Each medal
on each lapel signified a city or
campaign etched in Soviet military
history, each memory a part of the
collective wound left by million
battle casualties.

Nothing in Soviet modern
history is remembered with
greater passion and poignancy.

I don't think anyone living in
Moscow, even for a short time,
could fail to be impressed by the
sincere respect and admiration
shown by ordinary people for their
war dead. Russia never forgets the
people who serve her, and the
people who don't.

Every day, at every hour of the day, the teenage guard of honour watches over the monument to the dead of Stalingrad. They may have changed the city's name – in 1961 Stalingrad became Volgograd – but they have kept alive its memories. It's called a Hero City, and it paid heavily for the title: in this square as many as a thousand Russian soldiers died for every yard of their territory.

The guard alternates four times an hour, from early morning to late at night: only extremes of cold prevent the young people from parading. It is a ritual which will continue in perpetuity.

The teenagers, who are armed with model weapons compete for the privilege of forming the guard. They maintain rigid discipline at the memorial: anyone who goes too close, or is judged to be dressed inappropriately, is led away.

Last year a monument was erected with an inscription to Stalin – one of the few official structures which carries the name of the disgraced wartime leader.

Many in the city still revere him; many say they used to run into battle shouting 'for Stalin'. There is pressure to have the city named after him again – pressure so far ignored by the Kremlin.

I remember asking a war veteran how they could speak well of Stalin, after he had murdered so many thousands of his own countrymen. The reply is worth noting: 'We all make mistakes.'

10

God in Russia

I never discovered who she was, and at 3 am in the middle of the Orthodox Easter service it didn't seem right to interrupt and ask.

She had cared enough to travel forty miles from the Moscow city boundaries to the Orthodox showpiece at Zagorsk, Russia's religious centre. The town is a carefully guarded island of religious tolerance in a country committed by its government to atheism. Identity papers are checked at the gates to the churches.

Religion is considered acceptable for the elderly, but the Communist Party expects it to die with them. God is not for the young. Orders have gone out from the Kremlin to fight harder against religious feeling, but church tradition has proved resistant to state power and congregations remain static.

Christ, it seems, will rise again next year, and for many years to come, in Soviet Russia.

The Lutheran Cathedral in Tallinn, capital of Soviet Estonia. For many, Christ beckons in vain. The church faces the headquarters of the Estonian Council of Ministers, an odd juxtaposition. The day we visited, there was considerably more activity at the church than at the Council. But that, I know, is an illusion.

Twenty-five miles from Moscow, and the capital has disappeared. The noise and the crowds have gone. In the middle of a settlement of single-storey houses there's a working Orthodox church.

It's a hot Sunday afternoon in late August: the same sleepy Russia that the nineteenth-century writers captured so accurately. The pace of life is largely unchanged in the small rural communities. To some quaint and beautiful, to others stagnant and boring. The powerful keep their weekend retreats in this area, and the black official cars race through the countryside and disappear down unmarked tracks. I don't suppose they make much use of these little churches.

The door may be open, but you have to think carefully before going in. This church lies near the summit of the Lenin Hills. Like others it offers direct access to religion, and a direct break with the official atheist community.

It may not apply to old women – and the majority of churchgoers appear to be old women – but church attendance will automatically bar a citizen from official responsibility at local or national level.

That is a fact of Soviet life – and Soviet citizens go through that door well aware of the consequences.

Midnight in Zagorsk, the start
of the Easter service, and the
procession of clergymen and
churchgoers circles the chapel –
an ancient ritual enacted in
freezing temperatures.

The Orthodox clergy have found a place in Soviet society – or, more accurately, have been found one – and they keep to it. They are fully compliant with Soviet laws and policies, they support Kremlin statements on peace and disarmament and travel abroad, taking their government's message with them. Senior churchmen are sometimes awarded black official cars with drivers and sometimes host sumptuous banquets. As long as the Word of God stays within the boundaries of the church it is permitted.

It is hard to know where folklore
ends and religion begins. God is
bound up with the culture and the
language of the Slav lands. I have
seen known atheists holding
candles at an Easter service, and
even the Soviet leader Mr
Gorbachev was quoted as saying,
'God will not forgive us if we miss
this opportunity.'

   Russian culture is imbued with
the notion of One Truth, and for
many centuries that Truth was
God. In a superstitious, romantic
nation like Russia that idea passes
slowly.

The Orthodox Easter ritual. Outside a Moscow church the women nurse a lighted candle on the cakes they've baked themselves.

They were just out of sight of Moscow State University. Two Russias side by side; one in shadow, the other out in the open. The way it always was.